the Country Friends® Collection
CHRISTMAS CRAFTS

Holly
...loves to hang garland.

Kate
... still has her Easter decorations out.

Mary Elizabeth... knits & knits & knits hats & hats & hats.

OH·MY·AREN'T·YOU· CLEVER GIFT WRAPS

from the Country Friends®

Getting an idea should be like sitting down on a pin; it should make you jump up and do something. —E.L. SIMPSON

Fingerpaint!

Kids of all ages can't resist the pull of sticking their hands in the jar. Start with plain old tote bags ～ kraft or red or whatever color strikes your Christmas fancy. Smear on a white circle, add black dots for eyes & mouth and of course, a long orange carrot-shaped line for a nose … VOILÁ! Frosty bags!

Let the Kids

design your gift wrap. Turn 'em loose with big 11"x17" sheets of paper & colorful crayons... ask for Santa & Rudolph portraits, any holiday theme... stars, angels, snowmen, whatever! Then run down to your local printer or copy shop & run off color copies of your kids' masterpieces for unique wrappings... they'll feel like Rembrandt!

Presents

don't only belong under the tree. Embroider a name on a pillowcase in big, running-stitch letters ～ sew jinglebells on the case's borders and a homespun ribbon on the corner. Tie the case to the bedpost or a doorknob and wait for Santa to fill it with goodies!

JoAnn's GINGERBREAD BAGS

...FUN WRAPS YOU CAN MAKE IN A SNAP!

Here is what you need ～ JUST A SHORT LIST:

- ◆ KRAFT lunch Bags
- ◆ CANDY CANES
- ◆ WHITE opaque FELT-TIP OR BALLPOINT PEN

1. Fold the top of the bag down and decorate the flap like the roof of a gingerbread house with your white pen. Draw door & windows on lower half of the bag.

2. Punch two holes in the folded-down flap and slip a candy cane through to keep the bag closed.

P.S. ...don't forget to hide something yummy inside!

GINGERBREAD PAPER

is a good and easy country wrap!

Simply buy a roll of kraft-paper wrap (available at drug stores & discount stores in the mailing supply aisle) and wrap up all your boxes in it... Then take that handy white opaque pen and draw squiggles of "icing" on each side. Tie it up with good old jute and add a real gingerbread cookie on top for a tag ~ just pipe the lucky recipient's name on with icing.

Kate

WHAT LIES IN OUR POWER TO DO, IT LIES IN OUR POWER NOT TO DO. ~ARISTOTLE

Snowflake wrapping paper

- white butcher paper
- paper snowflakes (in lots of sizes!)
- acrylic spray paint (Holly likes silver & gold)

STEP 1 Unroll butcher paper ~ cut into sheets big enough to wrap gifts with.

STEP 2 Arrange snowflakes on paper.

STEP 3 Lightly mist paint over top of snowflakes.

STEP 4 Gently remove snowflakes ~ you'll discover a beautiful snowflake "stencilled" gift wrap! Let dry thoroughly before rolling up your paper.

Let the kids help you ~ just remember to work in a well-ventilated space.

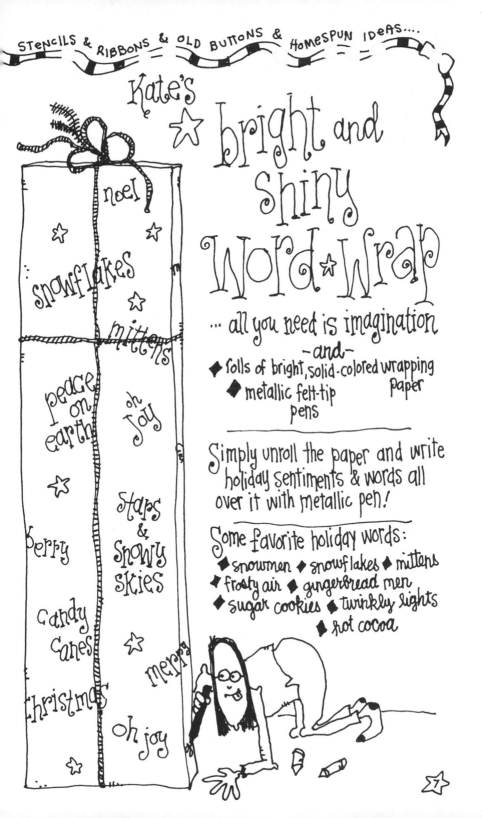

Kate's ☆ bright and shiny Word ☆ Wrap

... all you need is imagination
-and-

◆ rolls of bright, solid-colored wrapping paper
◆ metallic felt-tip pens

Simply unroll the paper and write holiday sentiments & words all over it with metallic pen!

Some favorite holiday words:
◆ snowmen ◆ snowflakes ◆ mittens
◆ frosty air ◆ gingerbread men
◆ sugar cookies ◆ twinkly lights
◆ hot cocoa

noel
snowflakes
mittens
peace on earth
oh joy
stars & snowy skies
berry
merry
candy canes
christmas
oh joy

☆ 7

Tuck little treats in...

Teeny Tiny old time Stockings

You'll need:

- 4 Teabags
- 2 pairs red or green tiny baby socks, prewashed
- paper towels
- buttons
- embroidery floss

1. Prepare some strong hot tea with the teabags in a bowl full of hot water. Let tea cool slightly.

2. Add socks one-by-one to the tea — let sit for 2 to 4 minutes. Tea will stain socks for an antiqued look.

3. Remove socks — blot dry with layers of paper towels. Lay socks on towels to dry.

4. Fold down top of each sock to form a cuff.

5. Stitch on buttons around cuff with embroidery floss.

Ideas! Raid your button box for neat old buttons, or buy new alphabet-letter buttons to spell out a name... Fill with tiny candy and use as a "place card"... make these using little mittens, too!

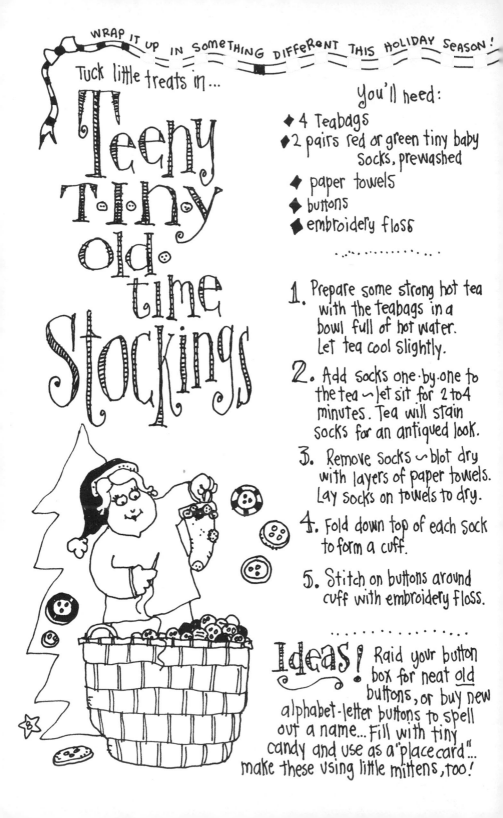

Vickie's ★ madcap, burlap, ★ shrinkwrapped, ★ snowcapped GIFT WRAPS

TUCK A PACKET OF COCOA, A HOLIDAY MUG, A SPOON & A FRAGRANT ORANGE IN A BRIGHT RED STOCKING CAP ... A FUN WAY TO GIVE A YUMMY GIFT.

TIE BIG INDIVIDUAL POPCORN BALLS UP IN CLEAR OR BLUE PLASTIC WRAP.... ADD A SILVER CHIFFON RIBBON WITH LONG RIBBON STREAMERS... NEAT NEIGHBOR GIFTS!

SPRAY-PAINT OR SPONGE GREEN PAINT ON AN OLD CLAY POT ~ RUB PAINT OFF WITH SANDPAPER. TUCK IN A RAGGEDY PIECE OF BURLAP AND PUT A TINY EVERGREEN IN THE POT... IT'S A NATURAL!

WRAP A BOX IN SHINY WHITE PAPER ~ GLUE HALF A STYROFOAM BALL ON THE BOX. DECORATE BALL WITH SNOWMAN BUTTON EYES & MOUTH ~ ADD A BRIGHT RED RIBBON BOWTIE UNDER HIS CHIN!

There is nothing greater than ENTHUSIASM.

~ Henry Moore

Winter Warmers to Share

Hot Cocoa Mocha

~ Mary Elizabeth's favorite gift from the winter kitchen!

3 c. hot cocoa mix
½ c. instant coffee
¾ t. cinnamon
½ c. mini marshmallows
Quart-size canning jar
    with lid

★ Blend hot cocoa mix, instant coffee & spice together. Pour mix into jar~ top with marshmallows.
Tie on a copy of these directions:

Hot Cocoa Mocha from your friend

serving instructions:

Add 3 tablespoons mix to ⅔ cup boiling water.

Vanilla Cream Coffee

...creamy, smooth & warm... a Christmas-time treat!

1 c. instant coffee
1·¼ c. powdered coffee creamer
1·¾ c. sugar
2·½ t. vanilla powder
Quart·size canning jar with lid

★ Blend all dry ingredients together. Pour mix into jar. Tie on a copy of gift tag (BELOW) with serving instructions.

★ Go ahead! make copies of the tags to tie on!

Vanilla cream Coffee from your friend

...to enjoy a cup, simply add 2 tablespoons of mix to 1 cup of boiling water.

Magic Reindeer Dust

...the perfect Christmas Eve gift for "believers."

Secret Ingredients!

* OATS (FOR ANIMALS)
* GLITTER
* PINT-SIZE CANNING JAR WITH LID

Secret How-To Instructions:

1. Fill jars with oats, sprinkling a little glitter throughout.
2. Top jars with lids and tie on a copy of "Secret Instructions for Magic Reindeer Dust" (below). You might glue it on jar, if preferred.

Make a Copy of this

Magic Reindeer Dust

Come December 24th, as Santa flies here from the North,
Here's what you do, it isn't hard ～
Just sprinkle this stuff in your yard...

The sparkles draw old Santa near
and oats attract his 8 reindeer...

Then just you wait ～ they're on their way

P.S. Happy Holiday!

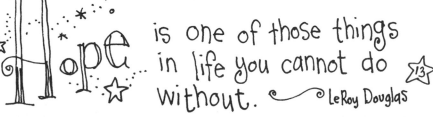

Hope is one of those things ... in life you cannot do without. ～ LeRoy Douglas

13

Mary Elizabeth's Cozy Christmas Fleece Ideas

Toasty & Terrific Scarves

Mary Elizabeth makes one for all of her friends... after all, every neck needs one!

- 1 yd. polar fleece (makes three 19"x36" scarves)
- cotton yarn in contrasting color
- needle (with eye large enough for yarn)
- scraps of felt
- embroidery floss
- buttons
- fabric glue

Step 1. Cut fleece into 3 strips (width-wise).

Step 2. Blanket stitch all around edges with yarn.

Step 3. Cut out fun shapes from felt ~ blanket stitch around edges using floss.

Step 4. Spread fabric glue liberally & evenly on back of felt designs and place on scarves. Add buttons ~ allow to dry.

* design ideas : blue fleece with yellow stars & moon .... red scarf with green trees & brown buttons ....

Soft & Snuggly Throws

... your friends will be snug as a bug in a rug if you give these for gifts!

- 1½ yd. polar fleece (this will make one 54"x 58" throw)
- cotton yarn in contrasting color
- needle (with eye large enough for yarn)

STEP 1. Using a blanket stitch, hand·stitch all the way around the polar fleece edge with yarn.

STEP 2. There isn't one- you're done!

¡Fleece Navidad!

JUST·a·THOUGHT:

Make smaller versions of the throws for the kids & babies in your family.

You might like to decorate a corner of each throw with a felt design, too ~ just like Mary Elizabeth's scarves.

Dig around in your button basket for interesting & beautiful buttons to sew on each project.

Sparkle ornaments

Have fun making different patterns with the glue... write names, make stars or stripes!

Color combinations are endless! Try icy blue or lavender-colored Christmas balls with silver glitter... frosty white ornaments with red designs... have fun.

...don't forget to lay down a newspaper before you start for quick and easy clean-up!

★ Matte-finish plain glass round ball ornaments (available at craft & holiday stores)
★ white school glue
★ silver & gold super-fine glitter

....

1. Dot half of ornament with round spots of glue to make polka-dot design.

2. Sprinkle ornament with glitter and allow to dry.

3. Repeat on other side of ornament.

Pretty!

CHRISTMAS

Yo*Yo

ornaments

... hang 'em on a mini tree in the sewing room. Top the tree with an old wooden spool!

* assorted fabric yo-yos (available at craft stores)
* tiny craft buttons
* glue gun
* embroidery floss (threaded onto needle)

. . . .

1. Glue a button onto the center of each yo-yo.

2. Attach an embroidery floss loop (for hanging) by threading the floss through the yo-yo. Knot floss in a loop.

Charming!

Yoyos will look cute sewn into a garland, too, for windows or trees!

Top off a special Christmas package with a length of homespun rag tied 'round the box and a yo-yo hot-glued on — just like a bow!

Kate's Snowman Topiaries

YOU WILL NEED:

* white acrylic paint
* small sponge
* 3" clay pot
* 3" styrofoam ball
* 2½" styrofoam ball
* toothpick
* orange acrylic paint
* whole cloves
* torn strip of homespun fabric
* tiny colorful buttons
* glue gun

...Tabletop guys to greet winter guests!

White acrylic paint

1. Sponge-paint the clay pot with the white paint. Let it dry.

2. Spread a thin line of glue around the bottom third of the 3" ball — place in clay pot & secure.

3. Glue the 2½" ball of top... see the snowman taking shape?

4. Paint the toothpick orange & let it dry.

5. Break off the tip of the toothpick and insert into styrofoam ⌣ that's his nose!

6. Press in cloves ⌣ the guy's gotta have eyes & a mouth, you know.

7. Now tie homespun 'round his neck for a cozy scarf and glue tiny buttons down his chest.

Make a whole family!

Love, and do what you Like.

— Saint Augustine

Family ✺ Calendar

...a thoughtful gift for Grandma.

YOU WILL NEED:

- blank one-year wall calendar (available at craft stores)
- white craft glue
- 12 pieces decorative paper
- fun edging scissors
- 12 color copies of photos or kids' artwork (you may need to adjust the size of your copies so they will fit the blank page above the months' grids)
- photo corners, stickers, rubber stamps, pens, markers, crayons ～ whatever materials you like to use!

1. Trim decorative paper to cover most of the blank page at top of each calendar month. Use those fun edging scissors!

2. Glue decorative paper to each blank page ～ this will be the background for your photo or artwork.

3. Trim copies of photos or artwork with edging scissors.

4. Place photo corners on each corner of the trimmed photo or artwork, then glue the whole thing onto the decorative paper for each month.

5. Embellish the calendar with bits of ribbon, stickers or rubber-stamped designs.

6. Using markers or crayons, label the month & days on each calendar grid. Be creative ～ and don't forget to draw a big star on family birthdays & special occasions!

"I absolutely ✺ love it!"

Vickie's Photo Boxes

... nostalgic gifts from the heart!

Have some fun going through family photo albums ~ and more fun putting those old pictures to good use!

★

Pull out favorite old pix and have them photocopied on a color copier. You can make them different sizes; reduce to 50% or 75%. Put as many photos on each copy as you can — you're going to cut them apart. Go ahead and get a few copies ~ you will use a lot with this good idea.

★

Vickie likes using copies of nostalgic old black & white photos ~ they look terrific on kraft-colored papier maché boxes.

YOU'LL NEED:

- PAPIER MACHÉ BOXES WITH LIDS
- ACRYLIC CRAFT PAINTS
- SPONGE BRUSHES
- FUN EDGING SCISSORS
- COLOR COPIES OF PHOTOS
- DECOUPAGE MEDIUM (CLEAR CRAFT SEALER)

Time is the soul of this world.

~ PLUTARCH

1. **P**aint the box & lid with sponge brush in the color of your choice. Let dry an hour or so, then apply another coat. Let it dry overnight.

2. **T**rim copied photos with edging scissors.

3. **D**ecide how you'll arrange photos on the box & lid. You can arrange them "randomly", at different angles for a fun scrapbook feel... you can also wrap some corners around the box edges.

4. **A**pply decoupage medium to the backs of photos one at a time, then apply to box ... just like you're gluing them on.

5. **O**nce you've placed all the photos, coat the box & photos with a coat of decoupage medium. Let dry completely. Add additional coats until all edges are filled in & box is smooth. Just remember to let each coat dry thoroughly before adding the next one.

an Idea or two:

• COVER A RECIPE-SIZE BOX WITH GRANNY'S FAMILY RECIPES & GRANNY'S PHOTO!

• PUT A KEEPSAKE TEA CUP OR OTHER RELIC TO PASS DOWN IN A BOX COVERED WITH FAMILY PHOTOGRAPHS—GIVE IT TO SOMEONE DEAR IN THE NEXT GENERATION.

Country Friends®

Joann fills clear glass bowls with peppermints, then tucks a pillar candle in the middle for a festive centerpiece. (small versions with votives make good place setting decor!)

Holly writes names on silk holly leaves with a gold metallic pen ∽ perfect gift-tags & place cards.

Mary Elizabeth volunteers to head up an afternoon of holiday crafts at her local school. (she's a brave soul)

Catch the Merry

Christmas Favorites

*Kate spends one whole Saturday in December in the kitchen with friends, baking dozens & dozens of dog cookies for a local animal shelter. All the kids in the neighborhood clamor to help!

*Vickie always stencils her kitchen window with a white wax crayon... the pretty snowflakes clean right off with window cleaner!

*Spotty strings jute across his windows & mantel and hangs up his Christmas cards with painted clip clothespins.

Christmas spirit!

pretty Christmas Cranberry hearts

YOU WILL NEED:

- UNFINISHED WOODEN FRAME, ANY SIZE
- GREEN ACRYLIC PAINT
- DRIED CRANBERRIES
- HEAVY FLORIST'S WIRE
- GLUE GUN

1. Lightly sand frame & paint. Let dry~ add additional coats if needed.

2. Trace opening of the frame onto a piece of scrap paper.

3. Draw a heart inside the tracing that touches edges.

4. Cut a length of wire to go around heart, leaving an extra inch.

5. Bend wire into heart shape, using your drawing as a guide.

6. Thread berries onto wire heart form. When you've almost reached the end, overlap ends & twist together gently.

7. Glue cranberry heart in the frame.

a THOUGHT to ponder:

Do you think Santa and Mrs. Claus leave their Christmas decorations up year 'round?

Fun homespun Garlands

... the fabric version of a paper chain!

YOU WILL NEED:

• 1" x 10" STRIPS OF TORN HOMESPUN FABRIC (a ½ yard of fabric makes about a 25-foot garland)

1. Tie first strip of fabric into a knot at the ends ~ this will make a circle.

2. Loop next strip of homespun inside first loop ~ tie ends into a knot. Continue until you have a long garland.

JoAnn's ☆Silly Snow★Men

Paper Dolls

Merry

When was the last time you made paper dolls? Get out your scissors... we're gonna do it again!

★

① Start with a piece of 8½" x 11" paper.... white is fine, or whatever's handy.

② OK. Fold it in half so you have a tall, skinny piece of paper 4¼" x 11". Turn it horizontally. Now start folding it accordion-style so it looks like this:

┌1³⁄8"┐

★ When you make that first fold, go in about 1³⁄8" (if you don't have a ruler handy, go this far)

├ ← - ← - ← ← - ← -┤ right edge of paper
first fold!

28

You're doing good!
③ Now hold the paper down, all folded up, and draw this silly snowman pattern on ....

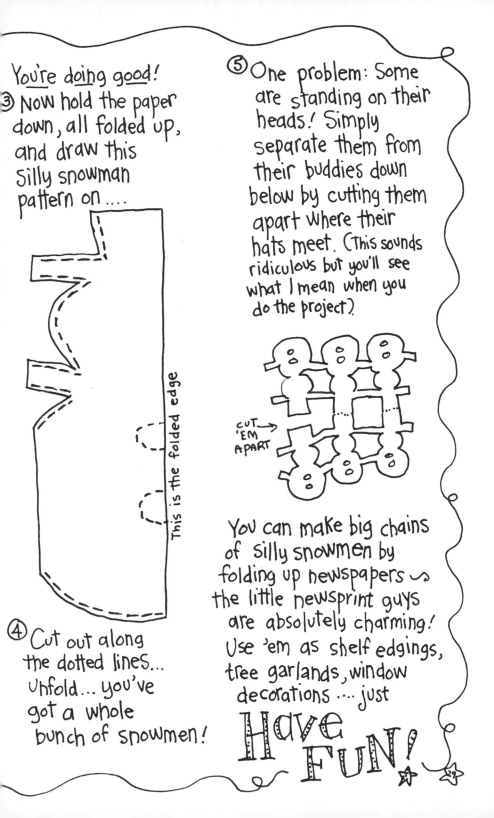

This is the folded edge

④ Cut out along the dotted lines... Unfold... you've got a whole bunch of snowmen!

⑤ One problem: Some are standing on their heads! Simply separate them from their buddies down below by cutting them apart where their hats meet. (This sounds ridiculous but you'll see what I mean when you do the project.)

CUT 'EM APART

You can make big chains of silly snowmen by folding up newspapers ~ the little newsprint guys are absolutely charming! Use 'em as shelf edgings, tree garlands, window decorations .... just

Have FUN!

eggnog is fine,
   fruitcake is dandy,
  but the best part of Christmas
              is

Christmas C·A·N·D·Y!

Layer penny candy in an old jar! Try red & green jelly beans... peppermints & butterscotch drops... chocolates wrapped in gold & silver foils. Tie on a candy cane & take it to a sweet neighbor.

With your trusty hot-glue gun, attach straight peppermint sticks to a mini chalkboard ~ just glue 'em 'round the edges. Then write guests' names on with chalk— cute and clever "place cards" for a holiday meal.
(Try this same idea on a big chalkboard and hang it by your phone for a handy holiday message center.)

Kate

Make an easy candy garland for trees & wreaths: simply lay out 6' of plastic wrap, cut in half lengthwise. Place peppermints or other Christmas candies about every 3" or so, then roll the plastic wrap over. Tie ribbons or homespun rag between each piece of candy. Make as many garlands as you need ↬ and try not to eat the candy!

Candy canes not only taste good... they look great!

Tie a bunch together with a pretty ribbon.... Stick a dozen in a plain clear glass.... Trim a package with one... and don't rely on just good old red & white; be brave and experiment with different colored candy canes!

The great thing about candy is that it has no redeeming social characteristics. Its only purpose is to please— to taste so sweet and so good that we simply have to go back for **More.**

— irena chalmers

The world belongs to the Energetic.

- RALPH WALDO EMERSON

CHRISTMAS

CHRISTMAS GOODIES For the COUNTRY FRIENDS©

ENJOY THE ENERGY OF THE SEASON!